WORKBOOK FOR

You Owe You

(A Guide to Eric Thomas' Book)

IT IS OUR PRIME DESIRE TO
SEE YOU SUCCEED AND
WE'VE DONE OUR BEST TO
MUCH SURE THAT THE
MESSAGE AND VALUES ARE
PASSED INTO YOU

ACHIEVING SUCCESS WITH THIS WORKBOOK DOES NOT RELY SOLELY ON US; INFACT, YOU HAVE SOME THINGS TO DO IN ORDER TO ENSURE OPTIMAL SUCCESS

NEXT TO THIS IS A CONCISE LISTING OF THOSE THINGS YOU NEED TO DO FOR OPTIMAL RESULT.

❖ It all starts from a sincere intention to truly imbibe the teachings of this book and its exercises. Don't compromise, don't deceive yourself.

❖ In that same philosophy of not doing it alone, you are advised to get a truly reliable person that'd be with you, guide and motivate you in this journey.

❖ Don't take any single thing here for granted, be serious with them and imbibe all values as a lifestyle.

❖ In the writing section, you are expected to completely pour out your mind, pain and positive decisions that'd lead to success.

❖ Keep in mind that everything here is possible and realistic for an average individual, don't believe otherwise because it's slow your path to succeeding with this book.

YOUR 1ˢᵀ DAYLIGHT ON THIS EXERCISE

USEFUL CHUNK FOR REFLECTION

Accept Yourself As You Are: The first step toward transformative empowerment is accepting yourself as you are.

FRUITFUL EXERCISES YOU COULD INDULGE IN TODAY

Think about the things that you're good at, the things that you're passionate about, and the values you hold dear.

FIX THIS DEEP INTO YOUR PSYCH!

Determine the areas of your life in which you may still have unrealized potential and become aware of any limiting thoughts that may be preventing you from moving forward.

OUTPOUR YOUR WORRIES
AND POSITIVE DECISIONS
HERE

_____

_____

_____

_____

_____

_____

_____

_____

_____

_____

_____

_____

_____

ALWAYS THINK OF THIS!

The first step towards awakening your
potential and locating your life's

calling is to cultivate a deeper understanding of who you are.

YOUR 2ND DAYLIGHT ON THIS EXERCISE

USEFUL CHUNK FOR REFLECTION

Discovering Your Life's Purpose is an Essential Part of Transformative Living Realizing your life's mission is an essential part of transformative living. FRUITFUL EXERCISES YOU COULD INDULGE IN TODAY

Think about the things that drive you, the things that intrigue you, and the kind of effect you want to have on the world.

FIX THIS DEEP INTO YOUR PSYCH!

Having a clear understanding of your raison d'être enables you to devise actions that will get you closer to achieving your goals and to make choices that will improve the quality of your existence.

OUTPOUR YOUR WORRIES
AND POSITIVE DECISIONS
HERE

_____

_____

_____

_____

_____

_____

_____

_____

_____

_____

_____

_____

_____

ALWAYS THINK OF THIS!

Establish a connection with your most fundamental beliefs, and visualize living a life that is in harmony with your purpose.

YOUR 3RD DAYLIGHT ON THIS EXERCISE

USEFUL CHUNK FOR REFLECTION

Establishing Meaningful Goals In order to provide a logical justification for each and every action you take, it is necessary to first establish meaningful goals.

FRUITFUL EXERCISES YOU COULD INDULGE IN TODAY

Create goals that are distinct, measurable, and attainable, and that match with your mission and beliefs.

FIX THIS DEEP INTO YOUR PSYCH!

The practice of transformative living entails breaking down large objectives into smaller, more manageable actions, which enables you to make progress toward your purpose in a way that is more deliberate.

OUTPOUR YOUR WORRIES AND POSITIVE DECISIONS HERE

_____

_____

_____

_____

_____

_____

_____

ALWAYS THINK OF THIS!

Create goals that are distinct,
measurable, and attainable.

YOUR 4TH DAYLIGHT ON THIS EXERCISE

USEFUL CHUNK FOR

REFLECTION

The cultivation of rational decision-making can significantly benefit from the practice of mindfulness, which has been shown to have a transforming effect.

FRUITFUL EXERCISES YOU COULD INDULGE IN TODAY

Living mindfully helps cultivate clarity, which in turn enables you to make decisions that are in line with your goals and principles.

FIX THIS DEEP INTO YOUR PSYCH!

Maintain presence of mind by paying close attention to your current thoughts and feelings, and choose your response carefully rather than responding on impulse.

OUTPOUR YOUR WORRIES AND POSITIVE DECISIONS HERE

_____

_____

_____

_____

_____

_____

_____

_____

_____

_____

_____

_____

_____

―――――

ALWAYS THINK OF THIS!

Maintain presence of mind by paying close attention to your current thoughts

YOUR 5TH DAYLIGHT ON THIS EXERCISE

USEFUL CHUNK FOR REFLECTION

Bringing Your Actions in Line with Your mission One of the key components of transformative empowerment is bringing your actions in line with your mission and values.

FRUITFUL EXERCISES YOU COULD INDULGE IN TODAY

Consider whether the things you do and the choices you make are in line with the direction you want your life to take.

FIX THIS DEEP INTO YOUR PSYCH!

Consider whether the things you do and the choices you make are in line with the direction you want your life to take.

OUTPOUR YOUR WORRIES AND POSITIVE DECISIONS HERE

_____

_____

_____

_____

_____

_____

_____

_____

_____

ALWAYS THINK OF THIS!

Bringing Your Actions in Line with
Your mission

YOUR 6TH DAYLIGHT ON THIS EXERCISE

USEFUL CHUNK FOR REFLECTION

Embrace the transforming Power of Self-Empowerment You should welcome the transforming power of self-empowerment into your life.

FRUITFUL EXERCISES YOU COULD INDULGE IN TODAY

Recognize that you have the ability to control the course of your life by taking responsibility for the choices and actions you make.

FIX THIS DEEP INTO YOUR PSYCH!

Adopt a development mentality and have faith in your abilities to accomplish success despite obstacles and fulfill your life's mission.

OUTPOUR YOUR WORRIES AND POSITIVE DECISIONS HERE

_____

_____

_____

_____

_____

_____

_____

_____

_____

———

ALWAYS THINK OF THIS!

Embrace the transforming Power of
Self-Empowerment

YOUR 7TH DAYLIGHT ON THIS EXERCISE

USEFUL CHUNK FOR REFLECTION

One of the key components of transformative life is the pursuit of both inspiration and growth.

FRUITFUL EXERCISES YOU COULD INDULGE IN TODAY

Put yourself in situations where you will be exposed to good influences, and actively seek out opportunities to learn and better yourself.

FIX THIS DEEP INTO YOUR PSYCH!

Inspiration is the fuel that keeps your passion and desire going so that you may follow your goal with unyielding resolve.

OUTPOUR YOUR WORRIES AND POSITIVE DECISIONS HERE

_____

_____

_____

_____

_____

_____

_____

_____

_____

_____

_____

_____

ALWAYS THINK OF THIS!

Seek Both Inspiration and Growth

FINAL NOTES BY YOU

WE'RE PROUD OF YOU,
YOU'VE COMPLETED THIS
EXERCISE!!

SUCCESS IS ON THE WAY….

DON'T EVER DISCARD THE
THIBGS YOU'VE LEARNT
HERE, COME BACK IF THEY
APPEAR TO BE FADING AWAY.

SHOW PEOPLE LOVE AND
SUPPORT, GIVE THEM
COPIES! IT'D GO A LONG
WAY.

Made in the USA
Monee, IL
10 January 2024